This copy of

The Crazy Crazy Facts Bag

belongs to

Lorna Gallacher

THE CRAZY CRAZY FACTS BAG

Janet Rogers

Illustrated by David Woodward

Beaver Books

A Beaver Book
Published by Arrow Books Limited
62–5 Chandos Place, London WC2N 4NW

An imprint of Century Hutchinson Ltd

London Melbourne Sydney Auckland
Johannesburg and agencies throughout the world

First published 1989

Text © Victorama Ltd 1989
Illustrations © Century Hutchinson Ltd 1989

Set in Baskerville
by JH Graphics Ltd, Reading

Printed and bound in Great Britain by
Courier International Ltd, Tiptree, Essex

ISBN 0 09 964910 1

Contents

Bags of Facts

Is it a book? Or is it a bag? The answer is both, because it's *The Crazy Crazy Facts Bag* — the book that can be carried around like a bag so that you always have hundreds of crazy, crazy facts at your fingertips.

There are all kinds of crazy, crazy facts packed into these pages to entertain and inform you. You'll find facts about food and animals, history and geography — even a special section of horrible facts to read when you're feeling brave.

I've had great fun searching out snippets of crazy information to include in these pages. Some of them may come in useful (like the fact that a hippopotamus can run faster than a man, which is very useful if you find yourself being chased by one!); most of them are totally trivial, and lots of them are very funny. But the best thing of all is they're brilliant when it comes to astounding your friends and convincing your teachers that you're a genius!

Like all good bags, there's room to put your favourite things inside because we've left some space at the end of the book for you to add your own crazy, crazy bits of information. So remember, next time you hear something absolutely amazing, grab your pen and pop the latest crazy fact into the bag!

Have a *factastic* read!

JR

Crazy Crazy
First Facts

All the crazy facts in this chapter relate to some famous and not-so-famous firsts!

Orville Wright, the first man to fly, was also involved in the world's first fatal aircrash.

Which two countries were the first to play each other at international cricket? England and Australia? India and the West Indies? No — the answer is Canada and USA in 1884.

Sir Christopher Cockerell, who invented the hovercraft, made his first hovercraft from a vacuum cleaner and an old tin can.

The first man to wear a top hat was arrested for doing so. The police said that his topper was likely to cause alarm to people of a nervous disposition.

The first medical thermometers were so big that you had to hold them in your mouth for five minutes before they registered your temperature.

In the first version of the Cinderella story, Cinderella's slippers were made of fur, not glass.

The first thimbles were invented about 300 years ago, and were called 'thumb-bells'.

The first baby to be born in Antarctica was born on 7 January 1978.

The Romans and the Spartans were the first people to play football, and by medieval times it was a very popular game in England. However, football as we know it was first played in 1869 in Britain.

Queen Elizabeth I owned the first wristwatch in England.

The first glass mirrors to be made in Europe were produced in Venice in the fourteenth century.

The first woman to take her seat in the House of Commons, Nancy Astor, was American by birth.

It's said that the first person in France to own a pet goldfish was Madame de Pompadour, Louis XV's mistress.

The first motorist to be booked for a speeding offence was accused of driving at 8 mph in a 2 mph area. The policeman who caught him overtook the speeding car on a bicycle.

The first recorded British earthquake occurred in AD 974.

The first newspaper was set up by Julius Caesar in 60 BC, and was called *'Acta Diurna'* — which translates from the Latin as *The Daily Happenings*.

The first pairs of false eyelashes were made in Hollywood. They were made by sticking human hairs to tiny strips of fabric, then sticking them to the eyelids.

The first queen to appear on English playing cards was Elizabeth of York, wife of Henry VII, who was queen at the time playing cards were first developed. Many modern playing cards still portray her face.

Shakespeare was the first writer to use the words 'hurry', 'lonely' and 'dwindle'.

Table-tennis was first called 'gossima' and tennis was originally called 'sphairisticke'.

The first person to invent the helicopter was Leonardo da Vinci, who designed one in the sixteenth century — long before anyone seriously thought about flying.

The first person to make sunbathing popular was fashion designer Coco Chanel. Before she started sunbathing it was thought very unfashionable, as only peasants and people who had to work in the open air got sunburned. Being pale was proof that you were rich enough not to have to work.

The dark side of the moon was seen for the first time in 1959, thanks to a satellite photo.

25 April 1792 was the day on which the guillotine was used for the first time. It was invented by Dr Guillotine as a way of executing people without causing unnecessary pain and suffering.

The first jeans manufactured by Levi Strauss cost under £7.00 for a dozen pairs.

The first elephant twins on record were born in Tanzania in 1976.

The first protective hard hats were worn by workers building the Vatican in Rome.

When Eau de Cologne was first invented it was intended to be used as protection against the plague. Then, when it didn't work, people kept using it because it smelled so good.

The first astronauts to go into space in Skylab were equipped with travel sickness pills — because apparently space travel makes lots of people feel sick.

The first city in the world to have one million inhabitants was London.

The first dog to be fitted with contact lenses was killed the following day when it tried to cross the road.

The first cookery lesson to be shown on television taught viewers how to make an omelette.

Mohammad is the most common first name in the world.

The first man to hit a golf ball on the surface of the moon was astronaut Alan Shepherd. For those interested in golf, he used a six iron and drove the ball more than 360 metres.

The first author to write his books using a typewriter was Mark Twain.

The first animal to be domesticated by man was the dog.

After he'd appeared in his first concert Elvis Presley was advised to give up music and become a lorry driver instead.

The first building in England to be fitted with a lightning conductor was St Paul's Cathedral.

A survey of eating habits revealed that when served a meal of meat pie, chips and peas, the first thing that 82 per cent of people taste is the chips, then the pie and then the peas.

Queen Elizabeth II is the only British monarch to have been born in a private house rather than a palace or castle or royal residence.

Sleeve buttons were first sewn on to the front of the sleeves of soldiers' jackets to prevent them from wiping their noses. As time passed and manners improved, the buttons were moved round to the back of the sleeve and were used for decoration only.

The first vegetable to be cultivated by man was the broad bean.

When Pepsi-Cola was first invented it was intended for use as a hangover cure.

The Romans first introduced the game of marbles to Britain.

The first Ford motor cars were made in only one colour, black.

Thomas Edison didn't just invent the first gramophone and the first light bulb, but he also invented the first electric typewriter.

The first gale warnings were issued in 1861.

The first British monarch to ride in a train, and to use the telephone, was Queen Victoria.

The first car ignition keys were introduced in 1929. Until then people had started their cars by turning a starting handle.

The first public toilets were opened in England in 1852, and during the first year only 24 ladies used them.

Flying became a more comfortable means of transport in 1931, when the first on-board toilet was installed.

Elizabeth Taylor was the first film star to be paid £1,000,000 for making a single film.

The ancient Egyptians were the first people to establish a 360-day year and a 30-day month. They were using this system in 4000 BC.

Prince Charles is the first member of the royal family to have ridden on the back of a killer whale.

The very first kind of Christmas pudding was a sort of soup with raisins and wine in it. It was known as 'pottage', from the French word for soup, *potage*.

Barbed wire was first developed in 1874 so that ranchers in the USA could section off their land without having to build expensive wooden fences or stone walls.

The first fish to be launched in space was a South American guppy.

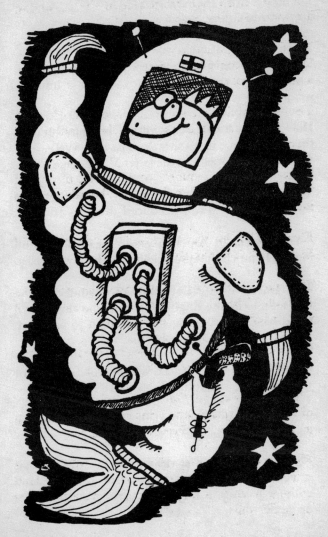

The first-ever Sunday colour supplement was included with the *Sunday Times* on 4 February 1962.

The world's first licence plates for cars were introduced in France in 1893.

The yo-yo was first invented in the Philippines, where it was not used as a toy but as a hunting weapon.

Do you know Beethoven's 'Fifth Symphony'? It's the very famous one that starts *da-da-da-dum*. Well, those first four notes spell out the letter V in Morse Code.

The first country to use paper banknotes was Sweden. They were introduced there in 1661.

Some drivers in America hated the first parking meters so much that they beheaded them with axes.

The famous aviator Louis Blériot was not only the first man to fly the English Channel; he also gained the distinction of being the first man to arrive in Britain without coming by sea.

Goal nets were introduced at a football match for the first time in Nottingham in 1891.

The first comma to appear in English punctuation was used around the year 1520.

The first bikini swimsuit was invented just a few days after the Americans had exploded an atomic bomb on Bikini Atoll, an island in the Pacific.

The first minute hands on watches were introduced in 1670.

There's a story told that sandwiches were invented by the Earl of Sandwich, who was so fond of gambling that, rather than leave the card table to have a meal, he asked for a steak between two slices of bread. The story may well be true, but the first sandwich seems to have been invented by the Romans, who called it an *offula*.

When asked to name a vegetable, the first that most people name is the carrot.

The first table-tennis balls were made of cork.

The first woman in America to wear toe-nail polish was film star Pola Negri.

The first public telephone kiosk was opened in Nottingham in 1908.

The first World Cup football contest was held in Uruguay in 1930, but because it was so far away only four European countries sent teams.

Queen Victoria was the first British monarch to have a state funeral. Before her time, kings and queens had been buried in quiet private ceremonies held at night.

The first recorded pavements to be laid in Britain were in Edinburgh in 1688.

Tanks first got their names when they were shipped to France at the outbreak of the First World War. They were packaged in crates that had been made to transport water tanks.

The first pillar boxes were invented and designed by the writer Anthony Trollope.

The first vegetable available in frozen form was asparagus.

Income tax was first introduced as a temporary means of raising money to fund a war in 1799. People hated it so much that it was abolished shortly after — but, sure enough, it was reintroduced at a later date and we've been paying it ever since!

The first balaclava helmets and cardigans were invented during the Crimean War. The cardigan was named after Lord Cardigan, who wore a knitted jacket over his uniform.

Popeye the Sailorman was the first cartoon character to have a statue erected in his honour. The statue was fastened to the plinth on which it stands by a mixture of cement — and spinach!

Crazy Crazy 'Fancy That!' Facts

This collection of facts got its name because I kept saying 'Fancy that!' when I discovered them. I hope you'll find them as surprising and strange as I do!

There are 3 miles of nylon yarn in the average pair of tights.

In Indiana, USA, there is a town called Santa Claus.

When Arabs shake their heads they mean yes.

A library in North Carolina, USA, banned children from reading the Bible without their parents' permission because of all the sex, violence, death and destruction described in it.

A computer scientist has estimated the intelligence of an IBM personal computer to be the same — or probably less — than that of a beetle.

The Doberman dog was 'invented' by Louis Dobermann, who wanted to create a fast and fierce guard dog. Sounds like the first 'designer' dog!

Every traditional circus clown has his own unique make-up design. He establishes this by drawing his face on an eggshell and when he dies the shell is broken.

One hundred and twenty drops of water are required to fill a teaspoon.

Our brains are 80 per cent water.

It has been reckoned that if Father Christmas were really to visit every house in the world on Christmas Eve he would have to travel at 50,000 miles per second, or faster.

The most popular holiday for British holidaymakers in 1988 was two weeks in Majorca.

The prudish Victorians were so shocked by the sight of women's feet and ankles that in some photographs these were cut out — so that anyone looking at the photo wouldn't get too excited.

The Statue of Liberty's nose measures 1.37 metres long.

If your parents ever moan about your fashionable shoes you may like to point out to them that in the Middle Ages there was a fashion for shoes with points between 15 cm and 30 cm long. Princes and rich people wore points 60 cm long!

Thirty-six million bars of Cusson's Imperial Leather soap were sold in 1988.

At school we're usually taught that Captain Cook was the first European to discover Australia, but there's evidence that at least three others had landed there before he did.

Some parts of the surface of the moon have been mapped out better than some parts of the Earth.

The uniforms worn by the Yeoman Warders at the Tower of London were designed during the reign of Henry VIII. Even older are the uniforms worn by guards in the Vatican City. Their outfits were designed by the great artist Michelangelo.

The word 'love', which is used to mean 'zero' in tennis, came from the French word *l'oeuf* which was French slang for zero because the symbol is egg-shaped.

The Japanese don't have names for the months of the year, they just use numbers.

Jeeps got their name because they were originally known as GPs. GP stood for general purpose vehicle.

It's traditional to serve a slice of lemon with fish because in the Middle Ages it was believed that lemon juice would dissolve any fishbones you accidentally swallowed.

The water in a kettle is hotter just before it boils than when it actually boils.

The first golf balls were made of leather bags stuffed with feathers.

Knowing that the Americans were upset that so many goods on sale in the USA came from Japan, the Japanese legally changed the name of one of their industrial areas to 'USA'. Now they can stamp the goods 'Made in USA'.

White rhinos are not white, they are grey. And white elephants aren't white either — they are grey with pink eyes.

If you have trouble when it comes to passing exams, take heart from Princess Diana who has only one 'O' level and failed five others — twice!

An eccentric French woman called Madame de la Bresse stipulated in her will that all her money should be spent on buying clothes for snowmen.

Bet you didn't know that earmuffs were invented by Chester Greenwood in 1877!

Because they live at such high altitudes, where the air is thin, Andean Indians have larger lungs than average.

You may think that darts is just a game people play in pubs, but it has a long and honourable history. Darts were originally thrown by medieval archers. When the enemy were too close for them to use their bows and arrows they would pull out their darts and attack them with those instead.

The words 'bungalow' and 'shampoo' come from the Indian language, Hindi.

There's no excuse for not reading a good book because, according to recent statistics, there is one library book for every person on Earth.

The weight of the earth is increasing each year by about 45,000 kg because of dust and debris falling from space.

In 1969 a survey undertaken in Morocco revealed that 12 per cent of the people did not know that man had landed on the moon. Many of those who *had* heard the news thought it was a practical joke, filmed in a TV studio.

It's often said that cats hate water, but some of them love it. The Turkish Van cat likes to go for a swim, as does the tiger.

Around the world there are 156 languages that are spoken by at least one million people.

Shoes worn on the right foot wear out more quickly than those worn on the left.

There are said to be 4000 different recognized knots.

In San Francisco there is a street named after a Chinese resident called Mr Wong. It's called Wong Way.

Thousands of church hymns have been written, but a survey has shown that the average churchgoer knows only 150 of them.

More women buy men's underpants than men.

Some maps of Russia used to show the capital city, Moscow, in the wrong place so that if guided missiles were aimed at it they would miss.

There are only two words in the English language which contain the vowels (A, E, I, O, U) in their correct order. They are 'abstemious' and 'facetious'.

If it rains on a bright moonlit night you can sometimes see a 'moonbow' — a night-time rainbow.

At the last count there were half-a-million men called John Smith living in America.

In Zambia there is a security van company that has equipped its guards with bows and arrows which, according to rumour, have poisoned tips.

In America they don't just celebrate Mother's Day and Father's Day — they celebrate Secretary's Day and Boss's Day too.

In America ice-cream sodas were banned on Sundays — so the ice-cream sundae was invented as an alternative.

On the island of Foula in the Shetlands they celebrate Christmas on 6 January, the date on which it used to be celebrated until Britain changed its calendar in 1752.

In the summer we often switch on an electric fan to keep us cool. But the fact is that far from cooling down the air, fans warm it up and then blow it around.

The average wink takes only about 0.1 of a second.

Every week 6000 new chemicals are added to the lists of the American Chemical Society.

If you live in London you may be interested to know that each glass of tapwater you drink has already been through nine other people.

In Japan the equivalent of our western Father Christmas is a woman.

You can check this fact for yourself; shirt buttonholes are usually vertical, but most pyjama buttonholes are horizontal.

An Exeter woman born on the day of Edward VII's coronation was christened Coronation in celebration of the occasion. Later in her life she met and married Mr Street — and became Coronation Street.

At international athletics meetings, races are always run in an anticlockwise direction.

Some types of bamboo can grow nearly a metre in the space of a single day.

The phrase 'nosey parker' referred to Archbishop Matthew Parker. He was well known for keeping his eye on everything that was going on and he also had a very long nose. Thus snooping became known as being nosey, and snoopers became known as nosey parkers.

Ballet fans admire the ease and lightness of the way ballerinas dance across the stage, but all those pirouettes and jumps are hard work. A principal ballerina may wear out three pairs of ballet shoes in a single performance.

Denim fabric, from which jeans are made, is named after the French city of Nîmes where it was first woven. It was known as fabric *de Nîmes*, which became 'denim'.

When you pull out a bathplug in Britain the soap bubbles swirl around in an anticlockwise direction. Pull out a bathplug in Australia, however, and you should see a clockwise swirl.

Haggis wasn't invented by the Scots; the ancient Greeks made it first.

Before she died, the religious leader Aimee Semple McPherson arranged for a telephone to be buried in her coffin so that after her death she could contact her followers and prove their belief in an afterlife. This was done, but when after seven years she still had not phoned them the line was disconnected.

In the southern hemisphere the man in the moon appears to be upside down.

In Siberia in the USSR it is so cold during the winter that people buy their milk frozen on a stick, like a giant ice lolly.

According to sales figures the average British family gets through 2 miles of toilet paper each year.

The first people in the world to use toilet paper were the Chinese. The Romans preferred to use natural sponges.

Next time you find a fly buzzing round your room you may be interested to know that it is beating its wings at a speed of almost 200 beats per second.

Historians reckon that Elizabeth I rarely ate a hot meal because the kitchens in her palaces were so far from the dining halls.

Ice is lighter than water.

Many people think that the Niagara Falls are the highest in the world, but in fact the highest are the Angel Falls in Venezuela.

The yard measure was created by King Henry I who decreed that it should be the distance from his thumb to the end of his nose.

Dry ice doesn't melt, it evaporates.

A survey in 1983 revealed that 43 per cent of adults in Britain did not have a holiday away from home.

Scientists studying hospitals discovered that there are more bacteria in an operating theatre than in the average living-room.

Tibetans have a rather unusual way of keeping warm. They rub their bodies with rancid yak fat.

Holly leaves growing at the top of the tree are less prickly than those growing at the bottom.

If you have ever used the phrase 'as cool as a cucumber' you may be fascinated to know that cucumbers really are cool. On a hot day the centre of a cucumber is about 11 degrees Centigrade cooler than the air.

Crickets can hear things through their knees.

Talk about selling coal to Newcastle — Saudi Arabia has imported sand from Scotland and camels from North Africa!

In 1983 someone added up the cost of all the gifts mentioned in the song 'The Twelve Days of Christmas' and calculated that if you wanted to surprise your 'true love' it would cost £6277.20.

There is a dating agency for dogs in France.

As well as recipes for spaghetti, Italian explorer Marco Polo brought back ice-cream from China.

Like human fingerprints, every zebra's stripes are totally unique.

People who have an IQ of 180 or more are literally one in a million.

The famous markswoman Annie Oakley could shoot a hole in a playing card that had been thrown into the air.

In Singapore chewing gum has been completely banned because it costs so much to remove it from floors, walls and furniture.

Pure gold is so soft that it can be moulded in the hands.

It's been worked out that one ordinary bucket of water could produce enough fog to cover an area of more than 250 km^2 with a blanket 15 metres deep.

The Chamois mountain goat has such tiny, nimble feet that it can stand on an area not much bigger than a 50p piece.

Crazy Crazy Food Facts

You'll need a strong stomach to digest these crazy, crazy food facts because some of them are very surprising — paritcularly if you're a vegetarian or fussy about the food you eat!

The oil in which tinned sardines are packed costs far more than the sardines themselves.

People in America drink more soft drinks each day than any other kind of liquid, including milk, tea, coffee and plain water.

Technically speaking, rhubarb should be classified as a vegetable and cucumbers and pumpkins should be known as fruits.

Everyone thinks that chop suey is a Chinese dish, but in fact it was invented in America.

The world's best-selling chocolate bar is the Hershey Bar, made in the USA.

Next time you have some Lea and Perrin's Worcestershire sauce on your food, spare a thought for the fact that it has been aged for two years before being bottled.

Chihuahua dogs were originally bred to be eaten by the Aztec Indians.

During his or her lifetime the average person in the West eats food equivalent to the weight of six elephants.

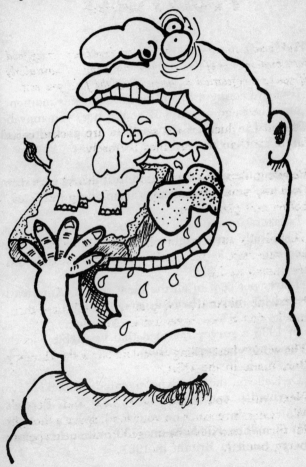

Kangaroo meat is very good for you because it contains no cholesterol, which can cause heart disease.

The best-selling savoury snack in Britian in 1987 was Hula Hoops. 392,857,140 bags were sold that year.

If you're eating a Spam sandwich at this moment, turn the page quickly. If you're not, you may be shocked to know that two million pigs are turned into Spam every year.

Among the ingredients used for making ice-cream is carrageen, which comes from seaweed.

Lobsters are naturally dark blue or green in colour. They only turn bright pink when they have been boiled.

Thirty per cent of all the meat sold in America is used for making hamburgers.

In 1986 a survey revealed that vegetable was the most popular type of soup.

Dr Kellogg, the man who invented cornflakes, also invented peanut butter.

1277 million Kit Kats and 730 million Mars bars were eaten in Britain in 1987.

Lettuce is the only common vegetable that cannot be bought tinned, frozen, bottled, pre-cooked or processed.

In 1979 bananas were the most popular fresh fruit in the USA.

The onion is the most widely used vegetable in the world.

To make one pound of honey, bees have to collect nectar from over two million flowers.

The biggest fish and chip shop in the world is in Yorkshire. It's called Harry Ramsden's.

Around 500 million snails are eaten by the French each year.

When tea was first imported to America it took a while for people to get used to making it. Some of them ate the tea leaves and threw away the water in which they had been boiled.

The most popular cheese in the USA is Cheddar.

In China, bear's paw is considered a great delicacy.

Tomato ketchup was used as medicine during the nineteenth century.

French people drink, on average, 100 bottles of wine each year. In contrast, the average Briton drinks just 13.

There are no turkeys in Turkey. Turkeys originally came from North America and they were called 'turkey' because when they turn sideways their head and neck looks — so it's said — like an outline of the Turkish coast.

One million cans of Heinz baked beans are sold every day in Britain.

The average person in Britain eats not three square meals a day, but six and a half! That includes all the snacks we eat throughout the day.

A 1987 survey revealed that people who go fishing are more likely to enjoy coarse-cut marmalade, Chinese food and Shredded Wheat than people who don't go fishing.

The British eat more sweets than any other nation, and the Scots eat more biscuits and cakes than anyone else in Britain.

They're so crazy about chocolate in America that there's a magazine dedicated to it. It's called *Chocolate News* and it comes in a brown cover which actually smells of chocolate.

Tomatoes were originally called 'love apples' and were thought for a long time to be poisonous. This was because they are red, and in nature many red berries are poisonous to man.

At the sound effects department of BBC radio they don't eat cabbages, they slice them with a sharp knife to get the sound of someone's head being chopped off.

1,200,000 chickens are eaten every day in the United Kingdom.

The Queen's dogs don't eat ordinary tinned dogfood. They have fresh rabbit, pork or chicken every day.

A survey on rubbish disposal revealed that in the USA people throw away about ten per cent of the food they buy.

One of the most popular delicacies in Ancient Rome was roast dormouse.

An American man from Maine, Massachusetts, was granted a divorce because his wife served him nothing to eat but pea soup.

In the state of Georgia in America there is a town called Bacon.

In Tibet they don't put milk into their tea. Instead they add a lump of yak's butter.

McDonalds sell more than three billion hamburgers a year.

In medieval times bakers were heavily fined if they gave short measures of bread, so they used to add an extra loaf to each dozen to make absolutely sure the weight was right. Thus 13 became known as 'a baker's dozen'.

The Spanish were the first nation in Europe to eat chocolate. It had been discovered by their explorers in South America. In Britain the first chocolate factory opened in 1720.

It was thought for many years that spinach was good for you because it contained lots of iron. Popeye's amazing strength was based on this belief. However, recent research shows that the human body can only absorb a little of that iron. So although spinach is good for you, it's not much better than many other vegetables.

Nearly three-quarters of the dates eaten worldwide come from Iraq.

So many eggs are laid by American hens each year that if you arranged them all end-to-end they would stretch around the Earth a hundred times.

There is a restaurant in Paris called the Tour d'Argent. It serves a very famous dish of duck cooked in its own juices. In fact it's such a famous speciality that every customer who orders it receives a card with the number of their individual duck on it, to prove that they've been there.

41

As one of her wedding presents, Queen Victoria was given a cheese. Nothing special, you might think — except that this particular cheese weighed half a ton and was 9 feet high.

In Iraq you can eat snakes on any day of the week except Sunday, when snake-eating is banned.

According to the results of a survey, at times of national trouble — like wars and economic recessions — people chew more chewing gum than at times of peace and happiness.

Bubble gum contains rubber. In fact, it was originally intended to be used as rubber substitute, and then someone realized that it tasted nice.

At a worm-eating contest in California, a man called Rusty Rice ate 28 worms.

You may have tried cheese made from goat's milk and yogurt made from sheep's milk, but did you know that, around the world, the milk of the llama, camel and horse are widely drunk?

We're always being told that drinking plenty of water is good for us, but a woman in Miami once drank so much water that her lungs filled up and she drowned.

Half the world's population survives on a diet consisting mainly of rice.

It's said that crocodile meat tastes like chicken — and possum meat is apparently just like veal.

There were no surprises when a study of the food that children like and dislike was carried out. Most of the children interviewed revealed that they loved chips and hated salad.

When Wrigley's launched their chewing gum, Juicy Fruit and Doublemint were the first flavours. Spearmint came later.

The world's first doughnut-hole machine was patented in 1872.

American Indians invented two of the world's favourite snacks — potato crisps and popcorn.

The poison cyanide is found in apple pips — but if you've just swallowed one there's no need to worry, because the amount is so small that it won't hurt you.

Buttercups are said to cause indigestion, so don't try eating them.

If you wanted to eat an ostrich egg you would have to boil it for 40 minutes. To hard-boil it would take about an hour and a half.

You use up more calories in the action of eating a stick of celery than are contained in the celery itself — so if you ate celery (and nothing else) you would lose weight!

Only in the last 150 years or so has food been served in 'courses'. Before that time all the dishes — sweet and savoury — were put on the table at the same time and everyone just tucked into whatever they could reach.

More tea is drunk by the people of the Irish Republic than anywhere else in the world, and the Swedes drink more coffee than any other nation.

Until 1700 all the world's coffee was grown in Arabia and no coffee plant was allowed out of the country. After that time some plants were smuggled out and coffee became widely grown throughout the world.

Today blancmange is a sweet, custard-style pudding, but when it was first invented it was savoury.

The best-selling ice-cream flavour is vanilla.

When baked beans were first put on sale they were sold with treacle sauce, not tomato sauce.

The Queen's milk is delivered in special bottles with her monogram on them.

The average Briton eats a large loaf of bread each week. Most of the bread we eat is still pre-packed white loaves; the best-selling sliced white loaf was produced by Sunblest, who sold 250 million in 1987.

Shredded Wheat, these days a popular breakfast cereal, was originally invented for people suffering from stomach disorders.

Many of us think of suet pudding as being a traditional English dish, but that is not so. Suet pudding was introduced from Germany in 1715.

The most fattening kind of fruit is the avocado pear.

When the Queen travels abroad she takes with her a supply of sausages from Harrods, Malvern water, Dundee cake and mint sauce.

Florida grows most of the world's grapefruit.

Champagne was invented by a blind monk called Dom Pérignon.

The original Cornish pasties had meat and vegetables at one end and jam at the other — main course and dessert all in one!

King Gustav III of Sweden believed that coffee was poisonous. He once ordered a criminal who had been sentenced to death to drink coffee every day, thinking that the man would die very quickly, but in fact he lived until he was 83.

If all the cans of Coke that are drunk each year in Britain were piled on top of each other, they would reach a quarter of the way to the moon.

Danish pastries do not come from Denmark.

Brussels sprouts are a good source of vitamin C when eaten raw, but once cooked they lose 90 per cent of it.

According to a 1984 survey, most people's idea of the ideal restaurant meal was prawn cocktail followed by steak and chips and chocolate gateau.

The state of Massachusetts in America has adopted the muffin as its official food symbol.

Lemons contain more sugar than strawberries.

The dish known as Bombay duck is actually made from curried dried fish.

One million tins of Heinz Cream of Tomato soup are consumed each day.

In Venezuela there is a tree called the cow tree that produces sap that looks and tastes like milk.

According to a survey carried out in 1987, strawberry cream was the favourite soft-centred chocolate.

In Japan the fu-gu fish is a great delicacy. The only problem is that it is extremely poisonous and has to be prepared very carefully by highly skilled chefs, who know exactly which bits of the fish it is safe to serve. Each year more than a hundred people die of poisoning when the cook gets it wrong.

There is a traditional belief that bread baked on Christmas Eve does not go mouldy, however long it is kept.

In Siberia during the last century, solid blocks of tea leaves were used as currency.

The sturgeon is a royal fish, and any that are caught in English waters have to be offered to the Queen.

In America crisps are called chips and chips are called fries.

When the QE2 set sail for the Falklands War she carried three million Mars bars for the troops. If they had been laid end to end they would have stretched for 320 km.

According to some nutrition experts, there are more nutrients in the cardboard boxes in which breakfast cereals are packed than in the cereals themselves.

Crazy Crazy Body Facts

If you ever doubted it, this chapter will convince you that the human body is quite simply the most complex and incredible structure ever known. A few of the facts are a bit startling, particularly if you're the squeamish sort, so don't read the following pages just after you've had a meal!

The average person in Britain has fewer than two legs!

We all shed our entire skin once every four weeks. It falls off in tiny flakes and creates dust. That's right — the dust on your bedroom floor is *you*!

The nail of your middle finger grows the fastest, and your thumbnail grows slowest.

Every morning in Britain, men shave off more than 48 km of beard.

The human body contains about 80,500 km of veins and capillary tubes.

Ten times as many men suffer from colour blindness as women.

When you blush with embarrassment, the lining of your stomach goes pink like your cheeks.

According to experts, a man weighing 68 kg would provide a meal for 75 cannibals. There is no record of a practical experiment to find out if this is correct!

There are more than a million tubes in the human kidney.

A human hair is a million times thicker than an atom.

In Germany a black eye is known as a 'blue' eye, and in France it's a 'poached' eye, because of its resemblance to a poached egg.

The average adult inhales about one pint of air with every breath they take.

It takes nearly a quarter of a million frowns before you develop a wrinkle.

There is a condition called 'double hemispherical action' which allows some people to write one thing with one hand, something completely different with the other and have a conversation with someone on a different topic at the same time. It's believed that Leonardo da Vinci, the great Renaissance artist and inventor, had this condition.

If you want to lose weight, walk rather than write — walking uses eight times as many calories as writing.

On average we have around 200 hairs in each square centimetre of scalp.

People over the age of 60 often use extra sugar and salt on their food because they have lost around 50 per cent of their tastebuds by that age.

If a pair of human lungs were unfolded and stretched out flat they would cover the area of a tennis court. But please don't try it!

Scientists say that girls sleep more soundly than boys.

When you hold a seashell to your ear it's not the sea you hear echoing back — it's the sound of your own blood pumping.

Traditionally it's been said that aristocrats have blue blood, but the only time anyone (or anything) has blue blood is if *(a)* they are being suffocated or *(b)* they are a lobster.

Have you ever wondered how influenza — commonly known as flu — got its name? It's because people believed it was caused by the evil *influence* of the planets and stars.

Human hair is so tough that if a hair was laid on a steel bar and passed through a steel rolling mill, the hair would leave an imprint on the surface of the bar.

The human skin weighs around 2.75 kg.

Eighty per cent of body heat escapes through the head, so in cold weather wear a hat.

The average human body contains enough fat to make seven bars of soap.

Some good news — 80 per cent of your liver could be removed and it could still function and eventually grow back again to its original size.

It's been discovered that people who take sleeping pills dream less than those who don't require them.

If you've got blue eyes they will become more and more pale as you get older.

It's easier to sing very high notes if you raise your eyebrows. Try it and see.

There is enough sulphur in the average human body to kill the fleas on a medium-sized dog.

A sixty-five-year-old man and a twenty-five-year-old woman are about as strong as each other.

Almost a quarter of all the bones in the body are found in the feet.

Two thirds of the weight of your body is water.

It takes 17 muscles to smile and 43 to frown — so save energy and smile!

Most people blink around 25,000 times a day.

The human brain is smaller, in proportion to body size, than the brain of a sparrow.

Four out of ten American women dye their hair.

French actor Pierre Messie could make the hair on his head stand on end just by thinking about it. The only time this happens to ordinary people is just after they have been struck by lightning.

Lots of people complain about their big feet, but few of them could have feet as big as Miss Fanny Miles of Ohio, USA. Hers each measured 60 cm long.

Blondes have more hairs on their heads than brunettes, who have more hairs than redheads.

Scientific investigation has shown that extroverts catch fewer colds than introverts.

More women require glasses for reading than men.

On average we each lose between 30 and 60 hairs every day.

Medical experts estimate that more people catch colds from holding hands than from kissing.

Blond beards grow more quickly than darker ones.

The vital statistics of the average Stone Age woman have been calculated to be 96 cm bust, 91 cm waist, 96 cm hips.

There are more bacteria in your mouth than any other part of your body.

Man is the only animal that cries when upset.

The first member of the royal family to be a blood-donor was Prince Charles.

It takes around a minute for blood to make a complete circuit of your body.

The average man spends about 145 days of his life shaving his face.

Only four babies out of every hundred are born on the day predicted by the doctor.

The human stomach can hold around 3 litres of food and liquid.

Muscles cannot push; they always pull.

The average human brain uses about as much electricity as a 10-watt light bulb.

If you are left-handed the nails on your left hand grow faster than those on your right — and it works the other way round, too.

About 13 million working days are lost each year because of backache.

When astronauts are in space they have to use a shaver that sucks in the bristles as they are cut off, otherwise the whiskers float around in the space capsule.

How supple are you? You're probably not as supple as the West Indian limbo dancer who managed to limbo under a pole only 16.5 cm from the ground! Try it for yourself and see how low you can get.

On average, the human brain weighs 1.35 kg.

Werewolves and vampires may really have existed. There is a disease called *porphyria* in which sufferers become very sensitive to light and can only go out at night. They also become very hairy and their faces develop an animal look. They are treated with a chemical extracted from blood — and as you probably know, both vampires and werewolves are fond of human blood!

There is enough carbon in the human body to make leads for 9000 pencils.

When he died, the body of the world's fattest man had to be transported to his funeral by a furniture van.

Banging your head against a wall uses 150 calories an hour — but it hurts!

One early beauty treatment for ladies with double chins involved hanging them in the air by a strap beneath their jaw. It's not reported whether this actually worked but it sounds very painful.

At this very second your skin is crawling with millions of microscopic organisms, some of which, if you could see them, look like strange elephants and dinosaurs. Don't panic and run off to have a bath; you can't get rid of these tiny creatures, and they are, in fact, vital to your skin and health.

The strongest bone in the body is the thighbone. It can support more pressure than a steel rod of the same size.

Human tears contain a soothing antiseptic substance.

On average, newborn babies spend 2 hours 13 minutes each day crying.

The acid in the human stomach is strong enough to dissolve a nail.

One ancient way of keeping teeth looking clean and bright was to clean them with urine. And only a couple of hundred years ago women used to wash their faces in urine because they believed it kept their skin soft and unlined.

If you're one of quadruplets, you might be interested to know that the odds against your mother having four babies at once was 1 in 600,000!

Snooker fans will be intrigued to hear of Henry Lewis, a man who could play snooker using his nose instead of a cue. Don't try it yourself, you might end up with a broken nose.

If you wanted to grow your hair long enough to sit on, it would take around six years.

In the time it has taken you to read this sentence 50 million of the cells in your body have died and been replaced by new ones.

Our sense of smell is much more important than our sense of taste; many of the things we 'taste' we in fact smell.

Several studies have shown that many slim people eat more than many fat people.

When you get up in the morning you are around 6 mm taller than you were when you went to bed the night before. You've also worked off around 300 grammes of weight during your sleep.

Try answering this question. Which kills people more quickly — lack of sleep or lack of food? The answer is lack of sleep.

Man is the only creature who sleeps flat on his back.

A Texas man was born without ears or even earholes, yet he was able to hear things through his mouth.

Most people turn over and shift around 40 times a night in their sleep.

Infants under the age of six months can breathe and swallow at the same time, which is why babies don't need to take a breathing break when they're feeding. Once past this age they have to stop every few seconds to get some air.

Wedding rings are worn on the third finger of the left hand because in ancient times it was believed that a nerve linked that finger directly with the heart.

Everyone's tongueprint is as individual as their fingerprints.

In America a man has successfully breast-fed his child. He managed this by taking a course of hormone tablets.

There is enough potassium in the human body to explode a toy cannon.

Every step you take requires 54 muscles to go into action.

The largest muscle in your body is the buttock muscle. The strongest is said to be the jaw muscle.

If you cut off the very tip of your finger, there is a good chance that it will grow back again.

A dog's sense of smell is a thousand times better than that of humans.

Your fingers and toes are the coldest parts of your body.

The emperor Napoleon's second wife could wiggle her ears and even turn them inside out.

After the age of 30 our bodies gradually begin to shrink.

When we are born, our muscles are only one fortieth of the size and power that they develop to.

Crazy Crazy World Facts

You don't have to be a great traveller or a geography genius to enjoy this chapter about our amazing planet. It's packed with fascinating facts about the Earth, the different continents and countries, and the crazy ways of the people who live in them. And, as you'll see, some of them are very odd indeed!

They don't greet each other by waving or kissing in Tibet — they stick their tongues out at each other.

In Britain black cats are thought to be symbols of good luck, but just across the Channel in France, black cats are considered to be bad luck.

The official language of India is Hindi, yet fewer than a quarter of the population speak it.

The South Pole is not a fixed point. It moves around every few years, and 450 million years ago it was where the Sahara Desert is today.

The Sargasso Sea is famous for the dense seaweed that grows there, and it's also interesting because it has no shore. It is entirely surrounded by the Atlantic Ocean.

Ninety-nine per cent of all the life forms that have ever existed during the Earth's history are now extinct — including dinosaurs.

There are as many rats in Britain as there are people.

The latest estimates put the age of the Earth at 5500 million years.

Spinach originally came from Iran.

American Indian peace pipes were often smoked through the nose, rather than the mouth.

The oldest inhabited city in the world is Damascus. People have been living there since 2000 BC.

There are more Jews living in America than in the State of Israel.

The greatest volcanic eruption in the world occurred at Krakatoa, Indonesia in 1883. It blew a 300 metre hole into the Earth's surface and the sound of the explosion was heard 4800 km away. It also caused massive tidal waves all round the world — there was even a tidal wave in the English Channel.

Half of the world's population live in just four countries — China, Russia, the United States and India.

We all know that birds migrate, but some butterflies do too. The painted lady butterfly travels 2500 miles from Africa and Asia to spend the summer in Europe.

If you're ever looking for a desert island to escape to, you might like to know that of the 3000 islands in the Caribbean Bahama chain, only 20 are inhabited.

At the last count there were more cars than people in Los Angeles.

If the whole history of the world was to be reduced into 100 years, the first man would have made his appearance on Earth less than an hour ago.

One in 25 British homes has a bidet, while in France the figure is one in four.

There are two and a half million rivets holding the Eiffel Tower together.

Statistics show that the average British person is more likely to get a divorce than to change their bank.

About 100 people die each minute around the world, but nearly 200 are born.

If all the world's mountains and valleys were flattened out to give a smooth area, every person in the world would have an individual space the size of five football pitches.

If you walked around 32 km a day, you could walk the circumference of the world in about three years.

The earth spins at 1669.7 km per hour.

The people of Iceland read more books than any other nation.

There are 27 words for 'snow' in the Eskimo language.

There are more plants and greenery growing in the world's oceans than on the land.

The entire continent of America could be fitted into Asia, with room to spare.

According to a magazine called *Fortune*, in 1987 the Queen was the richest woman in the world with a fortune valued at £5000 million.

It's difficult to keep a secret in the Arctic, because sound travels so well in the silence that an ordinary conversation can be heard 3 km away.

The world's first hospital for hedgehogs is called St Tiggywinkle's and is near Aylesbury in Buckinghamshire.

Denmark has the oldest national flag in the world.

More films are made in India each year than in any other country in the world.

Windsor Castle is the largest inhabited castle in the world.

Hungary exports more hippopotamuses than any other country in Europe!

In Ottawa, Canada, there is a law banning the buzzing of bees. And in Germany there is a law banning people from mowing their lawns between 1 pm and 3 pm on weekdays.

There is a city or town called Rome in every continent around the world.

Just 50 km beneath your feet the Earth's temperature is so hot that rocks are melted.

In summer lots of people wear straw hats known as Panama hats. In fact, they came originally from Ecuador and not Panama.

The members of the Japanese Imperial Family are the only people in Japan who have the right to drive a maroon-coloured car.

There are 22 reigning royal families in various parts of the world.

The ancient Roman week used to last eight days, and an ancient Egyptian week lasted ten days.

The Great Wall of China is the only man-made object that can be seen from the moon.

Greece is the world's leading exporter of natural sponges.

The Earth revolves around the sun at a speed eight times faster than that of a bullet fired from a gun.

The largest hailstones in the world fell in Seringpatan, India, in 1870. They were estimated to be as large as elephants.

In Africa, Masai warriors consider it polite to spit at each other when they meet.

More perfume is used in the USSR than any other country in the world.

American Red Indians used to name their babies after the first thing they saw when they left their teepee after the birth. That goes to explain the origin of names like Running Bear and Sitting Bull.

If the population of China were to stand in line and walk past you at a fast pace, the line would never come to an end because of all the babies being born and joining the line.

Land prices in Tokyo are so expensive that to buy enough land to build a telephone box you would have to pay £200,000.

Greenland is the largest island in the world.

The oldest surviving parliament in the world is the Althing in Iceland, which was founded in AD 930.

The world's most popular song is 'Happy Birthday to You'. What most people don't know is that it is still under copyright, which means that legally speaking every time we sing it we should pay the person who composed it a fee.

The best-selling book in the world is the Bible. The second best-selling book is the *Little Red Book* of Chairman Mao of China; he insisted that everyone in China should have their own copy, which explains why so many were sold.

The most common pub name in Britain is reported to be the Red Lion.

There are around ten times as many sheep in Australia as human beings.

It's been estimated that the world's chickens lay an amazing 400,000 million eggs each year.

The most common tree in the world is the Siberian larch. At the last count they made up almost 20 per cent of the world's forests.

The deepest lake in the world is Lake Baykal in Russia. At some points it is as much as 1.6 km deep.

The English language has more words than any other world language.

The largest iceberg ever spotted and accurately measured was larger than Belgium.

About two thirds of the world's population do not read newspapers, watch TV or listen to the radio regularly.

In Turkey, when someone dies the mourners wear purple, not black. And in China, white is the colour of mourning.

The most widely played game in Russia is chess.

In China they don't celebrate their birthdays as we do in the West. After the first year they only have a party every tenth year.

What is the most widespread disease in the world? Flu, perhaps, or the common cold? No, it's tooth decay.

When ancient Egyptians were in mourning they used to shave off their eyebrows.

One person in ten is left-handed.

Antarctica is the highest, coldest, stormiest and driest continent on earth. Not a good place to go for your holiday!

When we think of karate we immediately think of it as the Japanese national sport — but in fact karate was only introduced to Japan in 1916.

Believe it or not, the most common surname in France is Martin.

If you added together the areas of all the lakes in the world, the lakes in Canada would account for half of the total.

The Atacama Desert in Chile is the driest place in the world. As far as the records show, no rain has ever fallen there.

Turkish baths were not invented in Turkey; the Romans developed the basic idea first. And just for the record, Great Danes do not come from Denmark; they were originally bred in Germany.

In every country in the world, the average lifespan of a woman is longer than that of a man.

Although your birthday is a special day for you, it's also special for the nine million other people around the world who share it.

Mont Blanc is on a border, which explains why the eastern slope of the mountain is in Italy and the summit is in France.

The Earth's surface is constantly moving, resulting in two tremors or earthquakes every minute, somewhere around the world.

Portugal is the one great European colonial power with which England has never been at war.

If you need to look someone up in the Icelandic phone book you'll discover that they are not listed by surname but by Christian name.

It has been estimated that the average American carries five credit cards.

In 1985 it was estimated that if all the surplus grain in the world was to be put in plastic tubes 30 cm in diameter, it would stretch round the world no fewer than 600 times.

It is estimated that there have been only ten years in recorded history when two nations have not been at war somewhere in the world.

There is a street in Canada that runs for 1900 km.

Singing the Greek national anthem could take some time — it has 158 verses!

More Americans can trace their ancestors back to Germany than to any other nation in the world.

We all think of the world as being round like a ball, but it's not. It's flat at the top and bottom and it bulges in the middle, like a squashed orange.

The entire population of the world could fit on to the Isle of Wight — though there wouldn't be much room to move.

Although it would be very impressive to meet a crown prince of Arabia, it's probably not as difficult as you might imagine. You see, there are around 2000 crown princes of Arabia.

Birmingham has 35 more kilometres of canal than Venice.

Don't be fooled by its name — the Red Sea is the same bluish colour as most other seas.

The least salty sea in the world is the Baltic. The saltiest sea in the world is the Dead Sea, in Israel, which is so saturated with salt that it is impossible to sink in it.

More people are killed by bees than snakes each year, and the problem seems like getting worse as killer bees spread from South America northwards.

There are estimated to be 16 million thunderstorms throughout the world each year.

There are three times as many countries north of the Equator as there are south of it.

In the USA, more than twice as many cars are made each year as babies are born.

Each year the company that makes the Monopoly board game prints more 'money' than the American Treasury.

In New Zealand local telephone calls are free.

Anthropologists have calculated that in the majority of societies throughout the world, women do most of the work.

Crazy Crazy Animal Facts

If you're an animal lover you'll be fascinated by this collection of crazy creature facts. There are all kinds of animals here, from the bad-mannered llama to the sprinting hippopotamus to the extraordinary duck-billed platypus — which experts thought was a practical joke when they first saw it.

When Walt Disney's film *One Hundred and One Dalmatians* was released, thousands of people wanted to buy a spotty dog and this forced the price up by 400 per cent.

Cats cannot taste sweet foods.

Statistics show that, on average, city dogs live longer than country dogs.

Llamas are rather nasty animals. Not only do they have very bad breath, but if you go too close to them they spit!

It's not always cats that chase mice. A Somerset moggie called Ada was seen off by a vicious mouse that bit and squeaked at her.

Only male canaries sing.

The rough skin of sharks used to be used as sandpaper.

A Russian fisherman took his dog fishing, but it fell into the Pechora River and disappeared from sight. A few moments later the fisherman pulled in his net and discovered that he had caught an enormous pike — which had his dog's tail sticking out from its mouth. He cut open the pike's stomach and out struggled his dog.

Stroking cats and dogs is good for you — it makes your blood pressure drop.

According to statistics, the most vicious breed of dog is the alsatian. And surprisingly, number three on the list is the poodle.

A group of geese on the ground is known as a 'gaggle', but once they have taken to the air they are known as a 'skein'.

A kangaroo cannot jump unless its tail is in contact with the ground.

Polar bears are left-handed.

In Australia there are 'towers' built by insects called termites; some of these measure up to 6 metres high. If man were to build a tower of comparable height for his size, it would have to be four times the height of the Empire State Building.

In eight weeks a silkworm can eat 86,000 times its own weight. Wonder if it ever gets indigestion?

Crocodiles who live in the Sepik river in Papua New Guinea lay oblong eggs with white yolks.

There's one species of dog, the basenji, which canno
bark. It yodels instead, and it also washes itself lik
a cat.

If you would like to 'adopt' one of the elephants a
London Zoo it will cost you £6000 a year.

According to tradition, centipedes have 100 legs —
but that's not accurate. In fact, they can have a
few as 30.

A sledge pulled by ten husky dogs can keep up
speed of 12 km per hour.

There were no stray cats in ancient Egypt because
the Egyptians loved cats so much that all of them
were well fed and looked after.

Tarantula spiders don't spin webs.

We tend to imagine that all dinosaurs were huge,
but in fact many of them were small — some no
bigger than a hen.

Goats never close their eyes when they sleep. They
only doze, and the slightest noise wakes them up.

Moles and hedgehogs can swim well, as can
kangaroos and elephants.

Queen Victoria was a great dog-lover and in the Crufts show of 1891 won six prizes for her fluffy Pomeranian dogs.

The blue whale is so large that an African elephant could stand on its tongue.

When camels are born they do not have humps.

When the first English-speaking explorers saw the giraffe they thought it looked like a cross between a camel and a leopard — so they called it a cameleopard.

The ancient Macedonian king, Alexander the Great, had a wonderful horse called Bucephalus which only he could ride. He named an Indian city Bucephala in celebration of it.

When the Queen visited the island of Tonga in the 1950s, she was introduced to a giant tortoise that was said to have been on the island when Captain Cook visited it — in 1773!

An elephant's trunk can hold about 6.8 litres of water.

There were no rabbits in the British Isles until the Normans introduced them after the Norman Conquest.

An electric eel can produce 550 volts of electricity.

The largest bird in the world is the ostrich. It weighs as much as 48,000 times more than the smallest bird in the world, the hummingbird.

Horses, zebras and elephants keep themselves clean in the same way. They roll in the dust.

There is a fish that has been given the scientific classification *Boops Boops*.

The panda isn't a bear — it's a member of the racoon family.

It's been estimated that around 20 per cent of traffic accidents in Sweden are caused by moose.

The correct name for a group of crows is a 'murder'.

When a cat died in ancient Egypt it was often mummified — and when it was buried it shared its tomb with some mummified mice, so that in the afterlife it would have something to chase.

Male polecats love the smell of the plastic that is used to cover the leads and wires in car engines. Apparently it smells like lady polecats! Given the chance, they like to climb into the engine and chew the wires.

Dolpins are able to shut off the two halves of their brain independently, so they never close both eyes and go to sleep. They just shut down one half of their brain and one eye; the other is wide awake.

Hippopotamuses can run faster than a man — which is a useful thing to know next time you're chased by one!

Elephants are the only creatures to have four knees.

Sharks have to keep moving forwards to live. If they stop swimming they drown.

The duck-billed platypus is one of the oldest and strangest looking creatures in the world with a strange flat beak and poisonous claws. When the first platypus was sent from Australia to Britain, scientists took one look at the animal and decided that it was a practical joke.

Greenfly breed so quickly that one greenfly born on a Sunday can be a grandparent by the following Wednesday. It's enough to drive a gardener crazy!

Dogs sweat through their tongues and the pads of their paws.

Although they look fierce, gorillas never kill for food — they're vegetarian.

In America the US Navy has been training dolphins to check the sea for mines and bombs and also to carry out simple repair work on pipes. They can do it more quickly and easily than a man can.

Despite their long necks, giraffes have no more vertebrae in their necks than a man does. However, they do have very high blood pressure because it takes a lot of pressure to pump the blood all the way up their necks to their brains.

Next time you're stung by a mosquito it may help to know that only females bite. The males are vegetarian.

The only bird that can fly backwards is the hummingbird.

Guess where the world's only wild camels live? No, it's not the Sahara Desert — it's Australia.

There is no mention of cats in the Bible.

A 1981 survey revealed that the most popular names for cats were Samantha and Tiger.

Gorillas sleep for up to fourteen hours a day.

Crocodiles can't chew. To tear off meat, they grab their prey between their teeth and twist a chunk off by spinning over and over in the water.

Four out of five animals on the Earth are insects.

Windsor Safari Park has actually exported lions to Africa.

Koalas aren't bears — they are marsupials.

New Zealand was once the home of the Moa Bird, which was 3 metres tall. Unfortunately, it has been extinct for 400 years.

In Australia there are earthworms that grow to a length of 3 metres.

A scorpion can survive for three weeks if it is frozen in a block of ice.

If you leave a goldfish in a dark room it will gradually turn silver.

Fleas are the world's greatest jumpers. For a man to jump the equivalent height a flea can, he'd have to be able to leap over St Paul's Cathedral.

Snails can sleep for three years without waking up once.

A scientist has created a headless butterfly by chopping off the head of a caterpillar. Strangely enough, this does not kill the caterpillar. It develops a cocoon and turns into a butterfly as normal except for the missing head.

The oldest officially recognized breed of dog is the greyhound.

The starfish has an eye on the end of each arm.

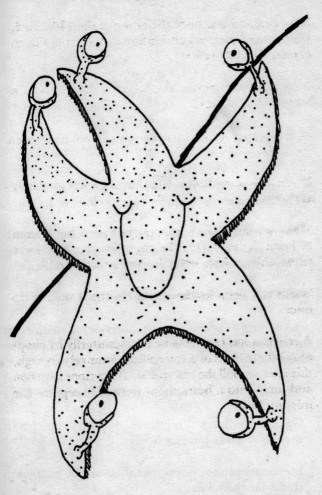

The kiwi, the national bird of New Zealand, has a beak so sensitive that it can feel worms wriggling about underground.

The chameleon's tongue is twice as long as its body.

There are no snakes in Ireland or New Zealand.

There are nearly 4000 species of beetle in Britain.

The last dodo in the world died in 1681.

According to scientists who study aerodynamics, it is impossible for bees to fly. It's a good thing the bees don't know that.

The most popular name for British dogs is Ben.

Caterpillars have three times as many muscles in their bodies as human beings.

Elephants cannot jump, but they can be trained to stand on their heads.

Everyone knows that the Queen loves dogs, especially corgis; but not so many know that she also has 'dorgis' — a cross between a corgi and a dachshund.

Many people think that a camel's hump contains water, but it doesn't; it contains fat.

Horses sleep standing up.

The largest eggs in the world are laid by sharks.

You might expect a camel's feet to be all hard and bristly — but they're not. Camels have very soft, silky feet. Next time you see a camel, tickle its feet and see!

Henry Egerton, Eighth Earl of Bridgewater, preferred dogs to people — so much so that his dogs had their own clothes and shoes and ate their dinner at the table with him each evening.

The common house fly can pass on thirty different diseases to man.

Frogs have no necks, and therefore cannot turn their heads.

Poodles do not moult like other dogs — they have wool rather than hair.

The most popular household pet in Britain is the dog. There are 6.3 million of them.

Snakes have no ears but they can hear by sensing sound vibrations through their tongues.

Bees die once they have stung someone.

Butterflies taste things with their back feet.

In July 1971 an American hen was reported to have laid an egg with nine yolks.

You can get rid of a scorpion by putting a drop of whisky on its back — it will sting itself to death.

Cockroaches can survive for several weeks after having their heads cut off.

An owl is able to turn its head in a complete circle.

Greyhounds can be identified by their noseprints, and registers of these prints are kept by the National Greyhound Association to prevent cheating at greyhound races. In Israel, cows are registered by their nose and tongue prints so that they can be identified if they are stolen.

A snail can crawl over a razor blade without slicing itself to bits.

Possibly the laziest creature in the world is the sloth. Some sloths move so slowly that plants grow over them. Running the sloth a close second is the dormouse, who spends almost six months of the year asleep.

Crazy Crazy History Facts

You may think that the world is a very odd place today — but wait until you've read these crazy facts from the past!

Henry VIII's second wife, Anne Boleyn, had five fingers on one hand — plus a thumb!

In 1925 the Canadian winter was so cold that the Niagara Falls froze over entirely.

William Wordsworth was Poet Laureate from 1842–1850. During that time he didn't write a single new poem.

Hundreds, perhaps thousands, of years before penicillin was discovered growing on mould, the Australian aborigines were treating their wounds with moulds that grew on their trees.

The 'Mona Lisa', probably the most famous portrait in the world, was first bought by François I of France, who hung it in his bathroom.

In 1666 the Great Fire of London wiped out large areas of the city and destroyed the original St Paul's Cathedral, but only six people died as a result of it.

Many royal princes in England and other countries had a whipping boy, a boy of about their own age who was beaten or whipped whenever the prince was naughty — because no one was allowed to smack a member of the Royal Family.

We think of King Richard I, the Lionheart, as a great British hero, but in fact he spent 95 per cent of his reign out of England and on the Crusades. Even worse, some historians believe that he practised cannibalism!

In 1898 the travel firm Thomas Cook made all the transport arrangements for getting British troops to the Battle of Khartoum.

Marble Arch in London was originally built outside Buckingham Palace, but it had to be moved because it was too narrow to allow the royal coaches to pass through.

The Chinese were the first to invent gunpowder. One hundred years after they developed it, the English used it for the first time at the Battle of Crécy in 1346.

The Italian flag was designed by French emperor Napoleon Bonaparte.

One hundred or so of the brave men who sailed with Christopher Columbus in search of America were criminals, freed from prison specially for the journey. No one else would go!

If you've heard of stories of the ancient city of Troy you may think of it as a huge and very exciting place — but the archeological evidence suggests that Troy probably just covered an area of about six acres. That's probably quite a lot smaller than your own town.

Have you ever wondered why pirates are traditionally shown wearing a gold earring? It's because all pirates wanted to carry enough gold to buy them a proper burial — and they carried the gold as an earring.

The doily takes its name from a seventeenth-century English draper who popularized them — Mr Doily.

According to experts, the price of coffee today is roughly the same as it was when it first came to this country in the seventeenth century.

In the eighteenth century some women used to wear huge wigs which were very rarely taken off or washed. When one woman removed hers, she discovered that a family of mice had built their nest in it.

The planet that we now know as Uranus was originally named Georgius after George III. Its name was changed in 1850.

In the early days of weightlifting, dumb-bells were made of bells that had had their clappers removed to make them 'dumb'.

Bonnie Prince Charlie escaped after the Battle of Culloden disguised as a lady's maid, in a frilly dress and apron.

It was dangerous to be a surgeon in ancient Egypt, because if their patients died they were liable to have their hands cut off.

The submarine was first invented in the early seventeenth century and King James I was the first monarch to go down in one. However, not many people were impressed with it; the British Admiralty reported that it was a 'damn silly trifling novelty that will never catch on'.

Perhaps the shortest war in the world occurred in 1896 when Britain and Zanzibar were at war for a whole 38 minutes.

James I banned playing bowls, bear-baiting and comedy plays on Sundays.

One of the greatest astronomers of all time was Tycho Brahé, who had his nose cut off in a duel. After that he wore an artificial nose made of gold and silver. Wherever he went he carried a box of glue in case it fell off.

Louis XIV of France took only three baths in his life, and none of them willingly.

There was no American national anthem until 1931.

Czar Paul I of Russia was so touchy about his baldness that he decreed that anyone who made any comment on it in his hearing would be flogged to death.

The Imperial State Crown, worn by British kings and queens at their coronations, contains a large ruby that was given to the Black Prince in 1367.

Three left-handers have worn the English crown; they were James I, George IV and Queen Victoria.

Historians reckon that the Black Death, a terrible plague that swept Europe in the thirteenth century, killed 42 million people — one in four of the population.

In the Middle Ages the unappetizing bits of an animal — the intestines, stomach and so on — were eaten by ordinary humble people while the rulers ate the best bits. This animal offal became known as 'umbles', and was often baked into a pie. All this goes to explain the saying 'to eat humble pie' when you have to crawl in apology to someone!

The girl's name Wendy was invented by J M Barrie, who wanted to include an unusual name in his play *Peter Pan*.

William IV of England was also William III of Scotland, William II of Ireland and William I of Hanover. Very confusing . . .

The first dinosaur skeleton officially recorded was discovered in the Oxford area in the seventeenth century.

Queen Mary II died in 1694 and barristers in the courts wore black robes to mourn her. They're still wearing black robes today!

Spain, or as it was originally known, Spania, means 'land of the rabbits'.

In February 1600 Will Kemp, one of Shakespeare's actors, danced a jig for 100 miles, all the way from Norwich to London.

Napoleon's wife, the Empress Josephine, loved roses so much that at her garden in Malmaison she grew every known variety.

The Chinese used to believe that eclipses were caused by a hungry dragon which tried to eat the sun. They used to bang gongs in an attempt to scare the dragon away.

When an ancient Roman raised his goblet in a toast to a lady, he was expected to drink one glass of wine for each letter of her name.

King Richard II married Princess Isabelle of France when she was only seven years old. By the time she was twelve she had been widowed.

11 BC was the last year to have a 30 February.

King Charles II used to rub the dust from ancient Egyptian mummies into his body because he believed it would give him 'ancient greatness'.

Mother's Day was invented by an American lady, Mrs Anna Jarvis, in 1906. During World War II American servicemen brought the custom to Britain where it took the place of the more traditional Mothering Sunday.

The largest solid gold object in existence is King Tutankhamen's coffin, which weighs an amazing 1104kg.

George V and Edward VIII kept the clocks at Sandringham half-an-hour fast so that they had an extra half-hour of daylight for shooting game.

Tuesday is named after Tiu, the ancient Saxon god of war, courage and the sword. In Henry VIII's day it would have been spelt 'Tewisday'.

The table fork was introduced to England in 1608 by Thomas Coryat.

If you've ever walked down the Embankment in London you may have seen a monument called Cleopatra's Needle. Unfortunately it has no connection with Cleopatra at all. It was put up in Egypt more than 1400 years before she was born.

Medieval monks used to call the loo the *Necessarium*.

Next time you cheer 'Hip, hip, hooray', you might like to point out to your friends that the words were originally uttered by crusaders when they stormed Jerusalem.

The Great Pyramid of Cheops in Egypt is so huge that you could put four cathedrals inside it and still have some room to spare.

Still in Egypt, the huge statue of the Sphinx is carved from a single chunk of stone. Modern pictures of it show that its nose has been badly damaged; this was done by Napoleon's troops, who used the Sphinx for their target practice.

When vaccinations were first developed in the seventeenth and eighteenth centuries they were considered so dangerous that they were tested out on criminal volunteers. If the criminals survived they were pardoned.

The Marquis de Pelier made a terrible mistake when he whistled at the French queen Marie Antoinette. He was locked up in gaol for 50 years for his rudeness.

Elizabeth I is said to have worn a new pair of gloves every day, and according to some royal experts Queen Victoria had new bloomers daily.

One ancient queen of Madagascar, Queen Ranavalona, banned her subjects from appearing in her dreams. If she *did* dream of them they were executed.

Despite its name Greenland is in fact a very icy and inhospitable place. It was named by Eric the Red, ruler of Iceland — which is not actually covered in ice — who wanted to encourage people to go and live in this new 'green' place.

For the big ceremony to celebrate the opening of the Suez Canal the Americans, who were organizing it, sent out invitations. One invitation went to the Swiss navy, and there were red faces when it was realized that, as a land-locked country, Switzerland has no navy.

H.M.S.
SWISS N

During the time of the Spanish Inquisition, the entire population of the Netherlands was once condemned to death for heresy. The sentence was not carried out.

The ancient Persian ruler, Cyrus the Great, sentenced a river to death after his favourite horse had been drowned in it.

Queen Victoria banned her royal train from travelling at speeds of more than 30 mph. When on one occasion she discovered that it had reached 40 mph she insisted that the driver was sacked.

Hitler's Nazi army was famous for marching in the goose-step style, but you may be surprised to know that the British army had used the goose-step long before Hitler came along.

The modern Olympics, based on the Olympic Games of the ancient Greeks, were started in 1896 and held in Athens. At the first games only nine nations bothered to send a team.

There is one German brewery, the Weihenstephen in Bavaria, that has been brewing beer for more than 900 years. When the Normans beat the English at the Battle of Hastings in 1066 the brewery had already been in business for 26 years.

Most of the racehorses we see today have Arab blood. They are known as thoroughbreds — and every thoroughbred horse is descended from just three Arab stallions that were imported to England in the eighteenth century.

The Hundred Years' War actually lasted 116 years.

There's a traditional story that the Roman emperor Nero played his fiddle while Rome burned, but it can't be true because violins weren't invented until centuries later.

It has been estimated that more than half the tea drunk in England in the eighteenth century had been smuggled into the country to avoid paying tax on it.

The tug-of-war was first recorded as a sport by the Chinese.

During the French Revolution, when the royal family were executed, kings, queens and jacks were removed from packs of cards because they were considered to be symbols of royalty.

The average life of a caveman was 18 years, and the Romans didn't do much better. Estimates have put their average lifespan at 22 years.

The game lacrosse was invented by the American Indians hundreds of years ago.

The world's first air raid occurred in August 1849, when bombs with pre-set fuses were dropped from hot-air balloons above Venice.

The ancient Chinese ruler Kubla Khan had 5000 astrologers at his court. Their job was to predict the weather and events — and if they got it wrong they were put to death.

In the early years of this century there was an attempt to make it illegal to sell and drink alcohol in America. This was called Prohibition, and it didn't work. A year after the Prohibition law had been passed the number of places you could buy a drink in New York had doubled!

There have been no new buildings erected in the Yugoslavian city of Dubrovnik since the nineteenth century.

In the Middle Ages pigeons supplied the major source of meat for most ordinary people.

During the reign of Elizabeth I there was a law which decreed that everyone except the rich was to wear a flat cap on Sundays.

In the eighteenth century the Puritans forbade their people to sing Christmas carols because they felt them to be out of keeping with the true spirit of Christmas.

Crazy Crazy CRAZY Facts

The facts in this chapter are some of the silliest the world has ever known. Most of them are absolutely useless except for one thing — they're ideal for amazing your friends and convincing them that you are an absolute genius!

According to ghost hunters, Britain has more spooks per square kilometre than any other country.

The island of Tonga once produced a stamp shaped like a banana.

During World War II several carrier pigeons were given bravery awards for their valuable work in delivering messages.

If all the frankfurter sausages eaten in America each year were lined up end to end, they would reach to the moon and back two-and-a-half times.

In Uganda in 1978 there were tens of thousands of reports that people had seen a talking tortoise.

A man called Robert Lindsay liked Land Rovers so much that in 1986 when his son was born he christened him Scott Land Rover Lindsay.

Many Victorians were so prudish that they would not place books by male and female authors on the same shelf.

The average pencil will keep writing for 56 km.

Conservative voters may be interested to know that the original Tories were a band of Irish outlaws.

Imelda Marcos, wife of the former president of the Philippines, owned a bullet-proof bra.

The durian is a fruit grown in some parts of Asia. It is said to taste delicious, but there is one drawback. It has a horrible smell, compared by some to the smell of rotting meat. In many places in Singapore and Hong Kong it is banned.

These days you can fly to the moon in a shorter time than it used to take to travel from Land's End to John O' Groats in a stagecoach.

At Christmas 1987 Woolworth's sold 7240 km of tinsel — that's enough to go round the M25 40 times.

It takes about 100 years for a tin can to rust away.

It is possible to boil water in a paper bag. It really is!

They don't sound like very safe drivers in New Zealand! In 1970 one driver there drove backwards for 175 km.

The Arabs have almost 1000 different words for 'camel' — wonder how they remember them all?

For 2000 years in India the distance a cow's moo travelled was used as a unit of measurement. People would say to one another, 'I only live seven moos away'.

If the Great Pyramid of Cheops in Egypt was pulled down, there would be enough stones to build a wall 2.5 metres high right around France.

It took Dumitru Dan six years to walk 100,000 km, with an average of 40 km each day. That's a lot of walking!

When George I became king of England he couldn't speak one word of English.

Many champion racing greyhounds eat cornflakes for breakfast.

When railway trains were first introduced, many people were worried about travelling on them. Some ladies used to hold pins between their lips in case gentlemen tried to kiss them when the train went through a dark tunnel.

In 1740 a cow was found guilty of murdering a farmer and hanged for its crime.

It's said by those who have counted that there are more acres in the county of Yorkshire than there are different words in the Bible.

A composer called La Monte Young has written a piece of piano music in which the pianist has to feed his instrument with hay and water.

If you ever get the chance to orbit the Earth in a spacecraft, you'll be able to see as many as sixteen sunrises and sunsets in the space of a single day.

Every hour that the Marks and Spencer chain of shops is open they sell one pair of men's underpants every three seconds.

Don't be fooled; the Century plant actually blooms every seven years.

According to London transport 75,000 umbrellas are lost each year on buses and tube trains. And British Rail reports that about 20 sets of false teeth are found on trains every year.

A crazy music teacher living in Paris named his children, Do, Re, Mi, Fa, So, La, and Ti after the notes in the musical scale. Then an eighth child was born — and was named Octave.

Tests show that elephants do have good memories. Experiments have proved that they have 70–100 per cent recall of things that had happened up to a year before.

Dr Who's evil foes, the Daleks, got their name when their inventor saw a volume of an encylopedia with the letters DAL-EK on its spine.

There are so many kilometres of road in America that if they were all joined together they would go round the world 150 times.

Not so long ago you could buy a rubber newspaper produced specially for reading in the bath.

In 1933 Mickey Mouse received more fan mail than any human film star.

If all the corks of all the bottles of wine made in France each year were to be balanced on top of each other to form a cork rope, they would stretch around the Earth ten times.

The average blue whale weighs about 4,800,000 times the weight of the average mouse.

How small can you write? Try challenging the record of C N Swift, who wrote the Lord's Prayer 25 times on an area half the size of a normal postage stamp.

Imagine that Russia, the world's largest country, was the size of a football pitch. In that case the world's smallest state, the Vatican City, would be around a quarter of the size of a postage stamp.

Next time you haven't got anything to do, try counting to a billion. If you count very fast and don't take too much sleep, it's been reckoned that you should finish in about 19,000 years' time.

Sean Connery, who used to play James Bond in some of the Bond movies, was once stopped for speeding by a policeman called James Bond. Really!

Cigarette lighters were invented before matches.

Amazingly enough, at the time it hatches, a baby crocodile is three times larger than the egg from which it hatched.

Weather experts, who have studied the weather records kept over the last 30 years, have discovered that Thursday is the wettest day of the week.

In Japan there is a place called O. In France there is one called Y, and Norway boasts a town called A.

Peanuts are used in the manufacture of dynamite.

Sausages were once banned from ancient Rome.

When the first Europeans arrived in Australia and saw kangaroos they asked the Aborigines what the animal was called. 'Kangaroo,' said the Aborigines — which means 'I don't know' in their language. The same thing happened when explorers went to the area known as Yucatan in Central America. 'What's this place called?' they asked the natives. 'Yucatan,' said the natives — meaning 'I don't know.'

It's illegal to hang men and women's underwear next to each other on a washing line in the American state of Minnesota.

In 1900 a prize was offered for the first person to make contact with a creature from space. There was one exception and that was Martians — it was thought they were too easy to contact.

At the last count, Madame Tussaud's waxworks museum was receiving two letters a week from people who would like to spend the night in the Chamber of Horrors.

Would you put your trust in a person who slept with the legs of his bed in bowls of salt water to keep evil spirits away? That's exactly how Benjamin Disraeli, Prime Minister from 1874–80, slept.

Yo-yos were once banned in the Middle Eastern city of Damascus because it was thought they caused droughts.

It's not on record whether Thomas Wedders was a nosey person, but he certainly had the longest nose on record — all 19 cm of it.

It's been calculated that the dead outnumber the living by thirty to one.

American dollars are made of special tough paper. If you fold a dollar 40 times in the same place it should not tear.

Doctors used to carry their stethoscopes under their top hats.

Mushrooms and crocuses are tough enough to break through concrete.

In King's Lynn, Norfolk, the Queen keeps a stable of 250 royal racing pigeons. Each of them wears a special leg ring with the initials ER.

King Edward VII liked his guests to eat well when they came to stay at his home in Sandringham. For breakfast there were sometimes as many as seven different courses! To make sure they had eaten enough, he used to weigh them before they went home to see how many pounds they had put on.

William Shakespeare, the greatest playwright the world has ever known, couldn't spell his name — or he couldn't spell it consistently, because his signature is spelt eleven different ways.

In France before 1785 handkerchiefs could be any shape, but after that a law was passed decreeing that they had to be square.

It was once illegal in England to have a middle name.

Archeologists working at Hadrian's Wall have uncovered a latrine that seated 20 people together.

In the Middle Ages a law was passed in England making it illegal to eat more than two meals each day.

Bad news. There's no rice in rice paper.

Human beings never naturally see more than one half of the moon because as the Earth turns the moon travels round, showing only one side. The only way of seeing the 'dark' side of the moon is in photos or using satellite pictures.

Telegraph poles confuse bears, who think that the buzzing sound of the wires is made by bees. Many bears have climbed the poles in their search for honey.

In Italy the number 13 is believed to be lucky.

During the Battle of Waterloo the Marquis of Anglesey had to have his leg amputated. His severed limb was given a full military funeral and buried near the battlefield.

Sales figures show that Japanese men use more deodorants and antiperspirants than Japanese women.

Europe is gradually sinking — that's why cities such as Venice are being increasingly eroded by the sea. If the continent continues to sink at the current speed, in 200,000 years the top of the Eiffel Tower will disappear under water.

To raise money, Elizabeth I put a tax on men's beards.

Crocodiles have to be polite — it's physically impossible for them to stick out their tongues.

A few years ago it was illegal to travel on a bus in Indiana, USA, within four hours of eating garlic.

All members of the Buddhist faith celebrate their birthdays on the same day — New Year's Day.

Men fall out of bed twice as often as women.

Castor oil is one of the best natural lubricants in the world — it's even used on jet engines.

According to those who have tried it, the only part of a reindeer that is worth eating is its tongue. The hippopotamus is a better prospect. When roasted it is said to taste like juicy pork.

In an attempt to cure his hiccups, one eighteenth-century man set light to his nightgown. He burned himself badly, but it's not recorded whether he cured his hiccups or not.

The Romans used a mixture of chalk and vinegar as a deodorant. Whew!

When you go to France remember that 'a.m.' actually means 'p.m.' because 'a.m.' stands for *après midi*, meaning afternoon.

Snoring can kill! People who snore very heavily occasionally swallow their tongues, which can be fatal.

Giraffes have such long tongues that they can lick their own ears.

In her later years Queen Elizabeth I must have looked pretty odd. She had lost all her teeth and stuffed a cloth in her mouth to fill out her cheeks when she appeared in public and she was also bald. Many women in her court shaved their own heads to follow the 'fashion' she had set.

There's a waterfall in Hawaii that flows *upwards!* The strong winds catch the water as it tumbles over the cliff and blow it back up again.

There are no reports of ferrets seen using handkerchiefs, but they can catch a cold in exactly the same way as we do.

A moment lasts around one and a half minutes, according to the old English time system.

The first trains used to attain speeds of 193 km per hour — but they had no brakes!

Late in his life, the billionaire Howard Hughes became extremely eccentric and odd. He disliked eating large peas, so he invented a special rake-like instrument through which only small peas would pass. Any that wouldn't go through, he didn't eat.

Crazy Crazy People Facts

There's an old north country saying that goes, 'There's nowt as queer as folk' — and when you've read these crazy facts you'll probably agree. Some of them have been taken from surveys, others are about the world's craziest crackpots and some are surprising facts about the lives of famous men and women.

A survey a couple of years ago showed that women are twice as likely as men to play bingo, but men are twice as likely to do the football pools.

You probably know some of the historical background to Mary Queen of Scots' life, but did you know she played a mean game of billiards and was also the world's first female golfer?

Studies have shown that a quarter of Americans and Europeans catch more than four colds a year.

A survey has shown that only one in a hundred married British men do the washing and ironing.

The Australian opera singer Dame Nellie Melba has had two foods named after her — melba toast and the delicious peach melba dessert.

That legendary Wild West hero Buffalo Bill was still alive when the first Western films were made and he actually starred in five movies, playing himself in each of them.

Roman soldiers who were stationed along Hadrian's Wall in chilly Northumberland used to keep themselves warm by stinging themselves with stinging nettles.

King Boris of Bulgaria was a great railway enthusiast who liked driving trains — and so was his brother. When they had to go on a train journey they used to argue in public about who was going to be the driver.

In *It Happened One Night,* a 1943 film, the actor Clark Gable took off his shirt and revealed that he wasn't wearing a vest underneath. In the weeks following, the sale of vests dropped by 40 per cent as men everywhere decided to wear nothing under their shirts.

Everyone knows that Casanova was famous for his love affairs, but it comes as a bit of a surprise to know that he spent the last thirteen years of his life working as a librarian.

The people of America sent one and a half tons of nappies to the Queen after the birth of Prince Charles.

A Korean child called Kim was able to speak four languages and do university-level mathematics by the time he was five years old.

Queen Victoria was the first woman to use chloroform to combat the pains of childbirth.

Attila the Hun, who conquered much of Asia and Europe, is believed by many experts to have been a dwarf.

Billionaire Howard Hughes was one of the richest men in the world yet he was so mean that at his luxurious home guests had to use a payphone if they wished to make telephone calls. Hughes also instructed his chauffeurs to drive in the middle of the road so that the car tyres didn't get covered in leaves and mud from the gutters.

Walt Disney, who created Mickey Mouse, Donald Duck and dozens of other cartoon favourites, admitted that he was not terribly good at drawing and gave up doing his own illustrations once his characters had become popular.

Soldiers in the Dutch and Norwegian armies are allowed to wear earrings.

Lewis Carroll, author of *Alice in Wonderland,* used to do all his writing while he was standing up.

When Prince Charles is introduced in pidgin English, a language still used in many parts of the Commonwealth, he is described as 'Number one fellah belong Missus Queen'.

In Canada scientists have found that women who eat salty foods and drink lots of tea and coffee tend to have boy babies, and those who eat eggs and milk tend to have girls.

The Queen uses black blotting paper.

We've all heard of the Egyptian queen Cleopatra
— but did you know that she was not actually
Egyptian but Greek? And, wait for it, her real name
was not Cleopatra but Auletes!

Geronimo, the great Apache Indian leader, was not
really called Geronimo. His real name was
Goyathlay, which means 'one who yawns' in the
Apache language.

King Mongut of Siam had 9000 wives. Just think
of all the birthday cards he had to send!

The Scottish man who invented the first two-wheeled
self-propelled bicycle was prosecuted for dangerous
driving.

Charles Blondin was the greatest tightrope walker
ever known. He once walked to the middle of a rope
suspended above the Niagara Falls and cooked
himself an egg on a stove there.

The Domesday Book reveals that there were more
than 28,000 slaves living in Britain in the eleventh
century.

One of the shortest people of all time was Pauline
Masters, who was only 58 cm tall. She died in 1895
at the age of nineteen. Her death was blamed on
her liking for alcohol.

Sir Winston Churchill's memory was so good that he is said to have been able to recite an entire Shakespeare play by heart.

An American lady called Marva Drew was surprised when her son's teacher said it was impossible for a person to write the numbers one to one million, so she got out her typewriter and started work. Five years later she got there!

Bing Crosby and actor Clark Gable both had big ears, and they both solved the problem by sticking them to the sides of their heads with tape.

Walt Disney is the only film producer to have been honoured by appearing on a postage stamp.

American film star Elizabeth Taylor is said never to throw any of her old clothes away.

King George VI, father of the Queen, was keen on embroidery and among some of the things he made was a set of 12 chair covers.

Corby Orr achieved fame when, at the age of five, he became the youngest golfer ever recorded to have scored a hole in one.

George Washington liked to be punctual but he wasn't keen on watches so he carried a portable sundial with him wherever he went. The only problem was, it didn't work at night.

If you live in Scunthorpe you'll be interested to know that your home town is named after Skuma, a squinting Danish pirate, who founded a settlement known as a 'thorpe'.

A woman in Russia is said to have developed X-ray vision after receiving a massive electric shock.

Lord Nelson, our most famous admiral, suffered from seasickness.

Have you ever wondered who invented the shoelace? It was Harvey Kennedy — so now you know.

St Cuthbert was famous for his skills at running and jumping.

It's said that only two men in the world know the secret recipe for Coca-Cola, and that if they both have to travel abroad, they go in different aircraft just in case one is involved in a crash.

Queen Victoria had to propose to her husband Prince Albert because royal protocol does not allow a mere prince to propose to a monarch.

The monasteries on Mount Athos, in Greece, ban women. Some of them ban female animals — even hens!

The only British prime minister to have been assassinated while in office was Spencer Perceval.

The Greek dramatist Aeschylus came to a very strange end. He was killed when a tortoise was dropped on his head by a passing eagle.

The philosopher Jeremy Bentham was a very odd sort of chap. He loved his pet cat so much that he knighted it and it was thenceforth known as Sir John Langborn. He was very fond of all his possessions and called his teapot Dick and his walking stick Dapple. When he died in 1832 he left his body to University College, London. You can still see his skeleton, dressed in his clothes and with his mummified head, on display in a glass case there.

Horror film stars Vincent Price and Christopher Lee were both born on the same date — 27 February.

Studies have shown that people who live in cities walk faster than people who live in the country. And when they have to queue, or at parties, the country people stand further apart from each other than city people, who are used to being squashed up together.

When he was a young and very poor artist, Pablo Picasso used to burn his own paintings to keep warm. These days his pictures are worth millions of pounds.

Good King Wenceslas was a real king of Czechoslovakia.

Madame Marie Curie, who discovered radium, died from radium poisoning.

Louis Braille, who invented the Braille system of reading for the blind, was blind from the age of three. His system was not originally intended to be used by the blind, it was devised so that the army could send messages to the battlefront at night — where it was too dangerous to light a lamp to read a written message.

The ballpoint pen was invented by Laszlo Biro — which is why they are called biros.

In 1986 it was revealed that more murderers come from Yorkshire than any other county.

Emperor Menelik II of Ethiopia had a favourite remedy for whenever he felt ill. He used to eat a few pages from his Bible. Unfortunately it didn't always work. When he was feeling particularly bad he ate the entire 'Book of Kings', but he died shortly afterwards.

Only one Englishman, Nicholas Breakspear, has ever become Pope. He died in a strange accident after choking on a fly which he had accidentally swallowed.

There is a theory that Napoleon Bonaparte may have been poisoned by his wallpaper. In those days a poisonous chemical called copper arsenite was used for the green colour on wallpaper. If it gets damp it can release a poisonous gas. Napoleon's room on St Helena was damp and it was also decorated in green wallpaper.

Women suffer from chilblains more frequently than men.

Some eskimos use refrigerators — not for keeping their food cool but to prevent it from freezing!

Only one in three members of the human race eats with a knive and fork.

There are more Italians living in New York than in Rome, and more Irish than in Dublin.

The Queen doesn't pay income tax and she doesn't have to put stamps on her letters.

Crazy Crazy Horrible Facts

When I was doing the research for this book I kept coming across facts that made me go 'Yuck!' — so I decided to put them all together in one completely horrible chapter. I hope you find some of them as disgusting as I do!

Can you imagine how horrible it would be to have a hat full of treacle pulled down on your head and over your eyes? Think of the treacle running down the back of your neck! Oooooooah! This method of mugging was used in the last century by the Molasses Gang, who attacked their sticky victims in the Manhattan area of New York.

Next time you have indigestion, try this ancient Carthaginian cure. All you have to do is to find a cow and rub its tail over your tummy.

Pot pourri, which usually consists of fragrant dried flowers and leaves which are used for perfuming rooms, actually means 'putrid pot' — not so nice, is it!

The first magician to saw a woman in half was the aptly-named Count de Grisley in 1799. Whether the trick worked or not, we don't know.

One of the strangest natural disasters is spontaneous combustion, when a person just explodes for no apparent reason. The best-documented case happened in 1938 when Miss Phyllis Newcombe spontaneously combusted while doing a waltz in a crowded dance hall.

On a chilly morning in December 1911 a large crowd gathered at the bottom of the Eiffel Tower to watch a man fly down wearing a special batwing cape. He had promised that it would allow him to soar like a bird, but unfortunately it didn't work. He jumped off the edge of the tower — and splat!

Mary Queen of Scots was very fond of wearing a watch shaped like a human skull.

George II met a horribly embarrassing end when he died after falling off a lavatory seat.

Have you ever heard the phrase 'mad as a hatter' to describe one of your nutty friends? The expresson dates from the time when hatters used mercury to make felt hats. The mercury was poisonous and affected people by making them go mad.

The explorer Sir Walter Raleigh, who brought tobacco and potatoes to Britain, was executed in 1618 when he had fallen out of favour with James I. His wife was naturally very upset, so she had his head embalmed and kept it in a red leather bag which she carried with her every day until her death, nearly 30 years later.

Experts have concluded that the population of North America is carrying around 200 million wobbling tonnes of excess fat. That's even more horrible when you think that, worldwide, one person in every eight is suffering from malnutrition.

In nineteenth-century Britain, people who tried to commit suicide and failed were sometimes hanged.

King Zogu I of Albania smoked 240 cigarettes a day — that works out at one every four minutes for 16 hours a day.

An entertainer called the Human Aquarium performed an act in which he swallowed three gallons of water and two dozen live frogs in one go.

Historians who have studied the food eaten in China in 1500 BC say that their favourite dishes included orang-utans' lips and swallows' tails.

In the fifteenth century, Scanderburg, ruler of Albania, once sliced two prisoners in half with a single stroke of his sword.

The Egyptians used to mummify their pet cats, and in one auction in 1890 180,000 of these feline mummies were auctioned. They were sold as fertilizer.

Peter the Great of Russia disliked beards so much that he sentenced any man who grew one to be shaved by force with a blunt razor. Ouch!

If you're twelve or under, you may be horrified to know that at least one third of the carpets made in Morocco are made by children under the age of twelve.

When the French king Louis XIV died his heart was preserved. Many years later it was eaten by William Buckland, the Dean of Westminster, who saw it sitting in a jar on the mantelpiece at a house he was visiting and mistook it for a pickled walnut.

It's easy to understand why so many people catch colds and flu when you consider that a really big sneeze reaches a speed a 166 km per hour. If you have flu, that single sneeze can spread 85 million flu germs a distance of 3.6 metres. Aaah-choo!

A man called John Morris had skin so stretchy that he could pull it up from his chest and over his head. And when he pulled the skin of his cheeks out to the side of his face, they stretched for 20 cm.

The bearded vulture is a horrible bird. When it can't find any dead prey to eat, it looks for a suitable victim and knocks it off a cliff.

Next time you're in Afghanistan you can go to watch a game of 'buz khashi', a sport in which Afghani tribesmen play polo using the head of a calf instead of a ball. Not so long ago it was played with a human head.

A lady in Los Angeles was so upset when her Pekingese dog died that she had it freeze-dried. Now it sits on the coffee-table in her sitting room.

The Russian ruler Ivan the Terrible was very pleased with St Basil's church, so he had the architect who had designed it blinded — so that he would never be able to build another to rival it.

The Roman emperor Claudius came to a horrible end when he choked to death on a feather which his doctor had stuck down his throat in an attempt to make him bring up some poisoned food he'd just eaten.

No one seems to know who invented the very first sets of dentures. Some were carved from wood, others were carved from ivory, and in America false teeth were made from elk's teeth, set in metal. Many people had problems keeping their early dentures in place and some of them went so far as to have their gums pierced so that their teeth could hang by hooks.

In 1685 the Duke of Monmouth was beheaded after leading a rebellion. It took five blows of the axe to chop off his head. After that was over someone decided that they would like a portrait of him painted — so his head was sewn back on again.

The writer Arnold Bennett decided to prove to his cowardly travelling companions that French tap-water was safe to drink. He swallowed a glass of it — and died not long after of typhoid, caught from the water.

People in Korea love eating snakes — so much so that they get through about 30,000 of them every day.

Some of the tribes in Papua New Guinea preserve their dead family and friends by smoking them above a fire and then propping up the bodies in their equivalent of a graveyard.

The first advert to be broadcast on Radio Luxembourg was for a laxative!

According to American researchers, around 15 per cent of the population of America chew their *toenails!*

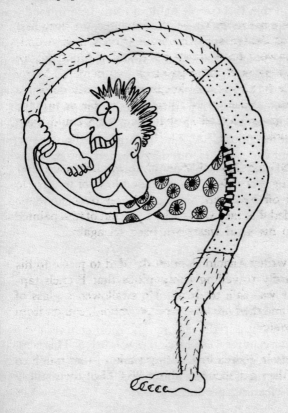

In 1738 Captain Robert Jenkins went to Parliament with a jar containing one of his ears. It had been cut off by the Spanish, and as a result of this England went to war against Spain. It has gone down in history as the War of Jenkins' Ear.

The Romans used to sweeten their food by adding lead. It didn't rot their teeth as sugar does, but they slowly developed lead poisoning, which damages the brain and prevents women from having babies. It's said that this simple habit of using lead in food was responsible for the fall of the Roman Empire.

The longest period for which anyone has been constipated is 102 days.

It's not very nice to think about, but the first head transplants have already been successfully carried out in Ohio, USA. The scientists used monkeys for their experiments, but they say there's no reason why it should not work for humans.

The Chinese eat dogs — one of very few societies which do so.

A few hundred years ago the most commonly used detergent for washing clothes was urine. This actually makes good sense because one of the major components of urine is ammonia — which is still used in cleaning products today.

In ancient India, and in this country too, one form of punishment for those convicted of certain crimes was to have their nose cut off. In India there were attempts to cover the spot where the nose had once been with skin grafts — possibly the first plastic surgery.

In the eighteenth century, people whose hair was going thin on top used to try to make it grow again by rubbing in bear grease.

Many people think that the greatest disaster at sea was the wreck of the 'unsinkable' ship the *Titanic*, which cost 1513 lives. This isn't, unfortunately, true. More than 7000 people were killed when the German ship *Wilhelm Gustloff* was sunk in 1945.

The library of the Vatican in Rome includes a number of very old books which were made using human skin.

Queen Elizabeth I was one of the cleanest people of her day, but even she was probably a bit smelly because she bathed only once a month — whether she felt she needed to or not.

In the fourteenth century more than 60 million people died of bubonic plague which swept Europe. Now the horrible news; it's still around! Eleven cases were reported in America in 1978, and two of them proved fatal.

Experts have shown that the sixth most common fatal accident in America is choking. More than 2500 people die each year when food gets caught in their throats. Bread and boiled eggs are among the major culprits.

When Alexander the Great died, his body was preserved in a big jar of honey. Something similar happened to the body of Lord Nelson. When he was killed at the Battle of Trafalgar his body was put in a large barrel of brandy to preserve it during the long journey home. Even more horrible, it is said that some of the seamen helped themselves to drinks of brandy from the cask while he was in there.

In Africa some tribes use large ants to stitch together their cuts and wounds. The ants clamp the wounds with their teeth, and then their bodies are broken off leaving their jaws in place. Very clever, *but* . . .

The French actress Sarah Bernhardt was renowned for her eccentricity. One of her strangest habits was sleeping in a coffin that was lined with the love-letters of her admirers.

The Aztec Indians of Mexico made regular human sacrifices to their gods. As if that wasn't bad enough, they also used to eat the remains of the victims — and historians now calculate that most of the Aztecs' protein intake came from this grisly source.

In China some children are allowed to smoke from around the age of four, and among Eskimo children the boys are taught to smoke a pipe at about the age of three.

Did you know that St Nicholas, whom we know better as Santa Claus, is the patron saint of thieves?

The body of Catherine de Valois, wife of King Henry V, was embalmed and buried in Westminster Abbey in an open coffin so that people could see her face. For his thirty-sixth birthday treat the diarist Samuel Pepys went along and kissed her. By that time she had been dead for more than 200 years.

When the English crusaders went to north Africa to fight the Turks they discovered that it was very difficult to get the bodies of dead crusaders back to England for burial. Not only were the bodies heavy, but in the heat of the long journey it was very unpleasant for those escorting them. Their solution was to take a large iron cauldron and boil the bodies, then bring back just the bones of the dead soldiers — much lighter to carry, and not so smelly!

If all the descendants of a single pair of flies survived for a period of five months there would be an amazing 335 trillion of them.

A tribe called the Lhopa, who live in Tibet, used to celebrate weddings by eating the bride's mother-in-law at the wedding feast.

Until only a hundred or so years ago in China, young girls had their feet bound in tight bandages to restrict their growth. This agonizing process gave them tiny but very painful and distorted feet. Chinese men thought they looked very nice, but many of the women could scarcely walk on them.

If you ever go on holiday to Florida, how about eating a juicy rattlesnake steak? It's served regularly there.

My Crazy Crazy Facts Collection

Add your own crazy facts in the spaces below!

My Crazy Crazy First Fact: _____

_____

_____

My Crazy Crazy 'Fancy That' Fact: _____

_____

_____

My Crazy Crazy Food Fact: _____

_____

_____

My Crazy Crazy Body Fact: _____

_____

_____

My Crazy Crazy World Fact: _____

_____

_____

My Crazy Crazy Animal Fact: _____

_____

_____

My Crazy Crazy History Fact: _____

_____

_____

My Crazy Crazy CRAZY Fact: _____

_____

_____

My Crazy Crazy People Fact: _____

_____

_____

My Crazy Crazy Horrible Fact: _____

_____

_____